"Never underestimate the power
you have to take your life
in a new direction"

-Germany Kent

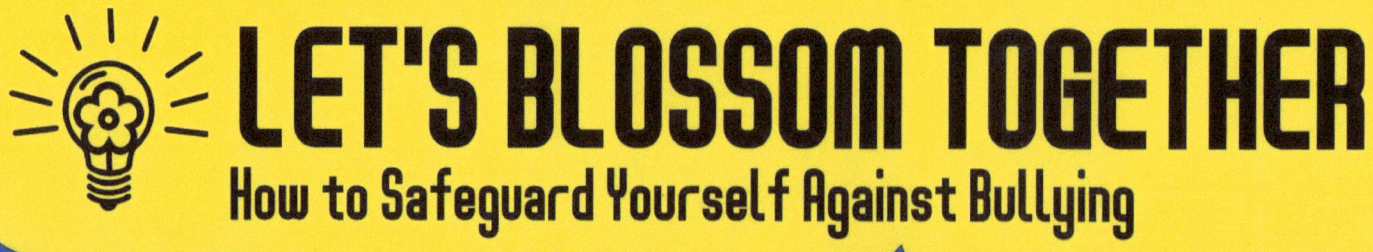

HOW TO SAFEGUARD YOURSELF AGAINST BULLYING
LET'S BLOSSOM TOGETHER
WORKBOOK

Copyright © 2017 Dara Wisdom and Empowerment Coaching / Reea Rodney

All rights reserved. This book or any part of it, may not be reproduced, in any form without written permission.

Printed in the United States of America
ISBN: 9780692989470

Written by Reea Rodney
Illustrated by Alexandra Gold
Designed by FindlayCreative.com

LET'S BLOSSOM TOGETHER
Workshop

Table of Contents

Page 4	Introduction
Page 5	About the Author
Page 6	What is Bullying? What is Bullied?
Page 7	Why do Children or People Bully?
Page 8	Who Are at Risk of Being Bullied? Are You a Target?
Page 9	How Do You Know if You are Being Bullied?
Page 10	Do You Bully?
Page 11	What to Do if You are Being Bullied.
Page 12	Important Tips for Parents
	Learning About Bullying Activities
Page 13	Activity 1- Are You A Bully Checklist Quiz
Page 14	Activity 2 – Have You Been Bully Check List Quiz
Page 15	Activity 3 - Examples of Bullying
Page 16	Activity 4 - Making Choices
Page 17	Activity 5 - Behavioural Goal Setting Sheet
Page 18	Activity 6 – Buddy or Bully?
Page 19	Activity 7 - Words to Live by Word Finder Puzzle
Page 20	Activity 8 - Being a Good Friend
Page 21	Activity 9 - Although We Are Different
Page 22	Activity 10 – No Bully Here
Page 23	Activity 11 - 5 Things You Can Do If You're Being Bullied
Page 24	Activity 12 – My Personal Declaration
Page 25	More by Dara Publishing and Strictly Essential Clothing

Copyright © 2017 Dara Wisdom and Empowerment Coaching / Reea Rodney

BULLY Here BULLY There, Do You Care?
LET'S BLOSSOM TOGETHER
Introduction

BULLYING: HOW TO SAFEGUARD YOURSELF

For too long until now, bullying has been a persistent problem that has refused to go away. More disturbing and alarming is how children under the age of 10 are so involved in picking at their peers and making them feel alienated. Like, no kidding!
Sadly, this aggressive behavior isn't inborn but an attitude that is easily picked up from society at a very fast pace, quicker than these kids can understand their school work. However, before a way forward can be pursued and implemented, some basic information about bullying has to be understood.

As a child, it is very likely you see evidence of bullying around you every day but sometimes confused on which is to be classified as bullying. Sometimes, you are left confused while trying to understand why for any reason a peer would deliberately pick on you or some other kid just to deliberately hurt them. You should know you are not alone and this workbook has just been put together to help you understand this social problem and how to appropriately react or respond when you are bullied or see someone else being bullied.

About the Coach / Author
Reea Rodney

Reea Rodney is a wife and mother of three wonderful children who resides in Brooklyn, New York. Originally from Trinidad & Tobago, a small twin island located in the West Indies, she migrated to the United States in 2006 in pursuit of a better life for her family. In addition, Reea is also an Empowerment Life Coach, Children's Author, Motivational Speaker, a Childcare Provider and a Medical Assistant.

Because of her innate passion and desire to help children, Reea was inspired to write children's books via her publishing company, Dara Publishing LLC. She wanted to assist not only the children who were under her care, but children all over the world. Fueled by this purpose, Reea became a Certified Life Coach. The result? Dara Wisdom and Empowerment Coaching. In addition, Reea aspires to be a positive voice of empowerment for children that she herself lacked when she was a child.

She seeks to educate parents and young children through her dynamic mini workshops and self-improvement workbooks. Topics such as Self-Esteem, Self-Love, Self-Celebration, Self-Confidence and Bullying are topics that Reea addresses through her programs. While most of these life skills are not taught in schools they are valuable to a child's overall wellbeing and development.

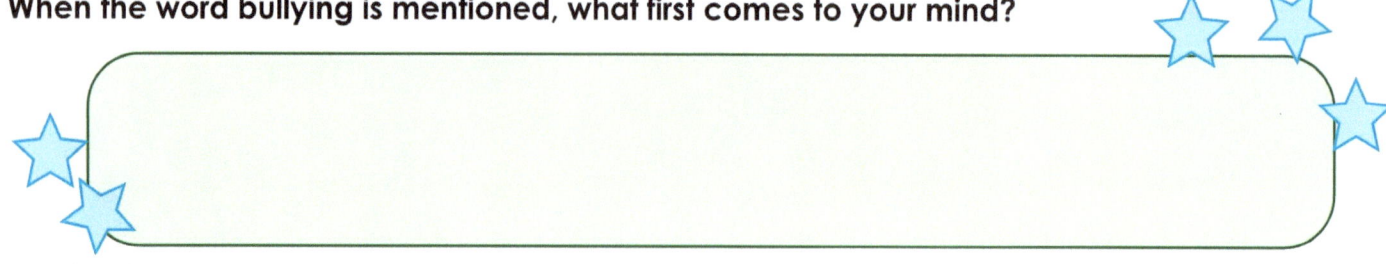

BULLY Here BULLY There, Do You Care?
LET'S BLOSSOM TOGETHER
What is bullying or bullied?

When the word bullying is mentioned, what first comes to your mind?

Bullying is a repeated negative behavior towards a person or kid that is seen as less powerful. This behavior is aggressive and could be verbal, social, physical, or psychological, and it is intended to cause distress, harm or fear.
Most often it is a display of power imbalance with severe consequences that could sometimes leave the person with a long-lasting setback to recover from.

Any child or group of children who are repeatedly picked on by another that flexes a perceived higher power is a Bullied. This attitude may be as a result of different reasons but always aims at giving a seeming authority to an individual or child to exert authority or harm another child.

Do you understand what a Bully is Yes or No? Can you explain in your own words What is a Bully?

Do you understand what is a Bullied Yes or No? Can you explain in your own words?

BULLY Here BULLY There, Do You *Care*?

LET'S BLOSSOM TOGETHER
Why do children or people bully?

Before any statement is made in regard to the question asked. Is there any way you think you or any of your friends have been bullied based on the definition of bullying mentioned earlier? **If yes, please write what happened.**

_____
_____

How did you feel?

_____
_____

Did you want to cry and run off to hide?

_____
_____

Did you feel lesser and got scared of making friends?

_____
_____

Did you wish that you would never be in the same class or on the same playground with them, or never see those bullies again?

_____
_____

If you don't mind, can you share a little of your experience?

_____
_____

BULLY Here BULLY There, Do You Care?
LET'S BLOSSOM TOGETHER
IMPORTANT FACT TO KEEP IN MIND

Some kids tend to take to bullying for so many reasons that could leave their victims asking an adult, like a parent, why? One thing to know is that sometimes bullies see more of the inappropriate behavior as 'fun' than 'mean.' And 'fun' is one enjoyable reward every kid would love to get from any activity they engage in.

ALSO...

Sometimes kids that bully others do so because they picked up the habit at home, an older sibling or even from their parents, which is very unfortunate. Other times these kiddies act the way they do because they are seeking attention or respect that has been denied them in their homes. It is very common to see a kid who has been neglected at home to lash out at others as a way to take away their frustration and any classmate or peer group perceived as weak, is likely to become their victim.

BULLY Here BULLY There, Do You Care?
LET'S BLOSSOM TOGETHER
Who's at risk of being bullied?

Who's at risk of being bullied?

Firstly, anyone can get bullied at any time. However, some risk factors could make a kid susceptible to bullying. Some of these risk factors include:

- Perceived as being different from the rest of their peer;
- Perceived as being weak or sometimes unable to defend themselves; Although, it has to be stated that some kids who can defend themselves, still suffer bullying. Those kinds of kids are called 'aggressive victims.'
- Looking depressed or exhibiting low self-esteem almost all of the time;
- Being less popular and unable to socialize freely.

How to know if you are a target of a bully?

OK, we have discussed who a bully is and some reasons why they display such character, but how would you know if you are a target of bullying?

The following sign indicators can reveal if you are a target of:

- Being persistently called mean names for fun;
- Being left out of groups deliberately;
- Being scared to go to school because of the way a fellow peer treats you or makes you cringe;
- And sometimes it could get to the extreme of being punched, kicked or hurt in any physical way.

BULLY Here BULLY There, Do You Care?
LET'S BLOSSOM TOGETHER
Do you bully?

You probably didn't see this coming, but some kids don't realise they are hurting others and what that means for them. And sometimes we also, don't know when we are hurting others through our bullying.

You are probably doing an appraisal of your actions towards others but still in doubt to tell if you are a bully or not.

Here's a checklist to help you know if you have been or are a bully:
- You gained fun or humor from treating a fellow kid in a way you know they don't like;
- You disregard people you think don't belong to your circle;
- You are very self-cautious of your popularity in school or among your peer group;
- You dare to gain attention and respect by every means.

Can you list three (3) ways someone can Bully?

1.

2.

3.

BULLY Here BULLY There, Do You *Care*?
LET'S BLOSSOM TOGETHER
What to Do if You are Being Bullied

So far you have been told what a bully is and why anyone would bully in the first place. You have also been told factors that could point out if you're a target of bullying or a bully yourself. Now, here's what you've probably been waiting for! How should you respond when you are being bullied?

Here's a few tips:
- Don't keep quiet about it. Talk to your parent or teacher.
- Don't think it's your fault.
- Be confident and just walk away with dignity. That way, you are taking away the bully's power.
- Don't skip school or fight back. Rather, act indifferent to the bully's meanness.
- Don't get tempted to bully back.

Can you list three (3) things you can do?

1.
2.
3.

BULLY Here BULLY There, Do You Care?
LET'S BLOSSOM TOGETHER
Important Tips for Parents

As a parent, you could also be of great assistance to help shield your child from the effects of bullying.

The following are ways you could safeguard your child from bullying:
- Watch for signs that tell you that your child is being bullied;
- Encourage your child to be more open with you about what happens in school or elsewhere;
- Reach out to your child's teacher and let him or her know what's going on and how displeased you are about your child feeling unsafe in school;
- Train your child to exhibit positive body language;
- Don't think they are too young to learn. Teach them how respond appropriately to a bully in a strong and firm voice. Practice a script, if need be – he or she is your child, after all, you don't want to see them get hurt;
- Pay attention to your child. You should be their first confidant;
- Try and praise their progress when your child tell you how they defused a harasser;
- Help your child grow from the experience; if the bullying is severe, seek the support of a counsellor.

Activity 1
Are You A Bully Checklist Quiz

Read each of the following questions and check the box next to anything that you may have experienced. If you need help, ask your mom or dad!

The "Are You A Bully?" Check-List

✓	
	1. Have you ever laughed at someone when they made a mistake?
	2. Have you ever laughed at another person that was teased by someone else?
	3. Have you ever teased someone by calling them a negative name?
	4. Have you bullied someone, whether it was a little bit or a lot?
	5. Have you ever bullied someone in your entire life?
	6. Have you ever bullied someone after they bullied you, to get even?
	7. Have you ever bullied a brother or sister or another family member?
	8. Have you ever fought with your friends or another student?
	9. Have you ever, together with a group of students, became angry at a person, called them names or even fought with them?
	10. Have you ever thought about calling somebody's name or fighting with them because they had done something mean to you?

Activity 2
Have You Been Bullied Quiz

Read each of the following questions and check the box next to anything that you may have experienced. If you need help, ask a grown-up.

✓ The "Have You Been Bullied?" Check-List

1. Have you ever been afraid of other kids on the playground?
2. Have you ever been bullied by a brother or sister, or other family member?
3. Have you ever been called names by other students or friends?
4. Did you ever get into a fight with other students?
5. Have you ever felt bad after other students said something negative about you?
6. Have you ever felt that other kids ignored you?
7. Have you ever felt that the students laugh at you for something you couldn't change?
8. Have you ever felt that some people have treated you much worse than others around you?
9. Have you ever not wanted to go to school because the students have been treating you badly?
10. Have you ever felt bullied in any way, shape or form by a group of older kids from another grade?

Activity 3
Examples of Bullying

Now that you have learned about Bullying can you give some examples of Bullying below?

Bullying is when someone keeps doing or saying things to have power over another person. Bullying can cover many forms of unacceptable behaviour.

Name three (3) ways bullies threaten other people.

1.

2.

3.

2 How do you feel when you are being bullied?

Write down three (3) reasons why some people bully others.

1.

2.

3.

Activity 4
Making Choices

This activity is designed to help you identify some good and bad choices, so that you can make better decisions while in school, home or with your peers.

Write the choices from below in the list they belong to. Cross the choice off the list once you have used it.

Good Choice	Bad Choice

Pushing / Teasing / Bullying / Helping / Sharing / Teamwork
Playing Nicely, / Say Mean Words / Showing Kindness / Hurting Others

Page 16   Copyright © 2017 Dara Wisdom and Empowerment Coaching / Reea Rodney

Activity 5
Behavioural Goal Setting Sheet

This self-improvement worksheet, once completed, establishes what steps you need to take to achieve your goal. This activity requires you to take ownership of how you can improve yourself or reach a goal.

It can be used for:
- Behavior modification
- Self-regulation
- Goal setting

Example: If you are having problems communicating or playing with children or one child in particular in class, by completing this worksheet and setting goals you can work towards improving that behavior.

Name: _____

Date: _____

Currently I can:
_____
_____
_____

I need to improve:
_____
_____
_____

My goal is to:
_____
_____
_____

List ways to reach your goal:
_____
_____
_____
_____

I will achieve the goal by this date: _____

Activity 6
Buddy or Bully?

Learning how to treat others with respect, in addition to improving your communication skills is a huge part of being a Buddy. Use this worksheet to help guide a discussion of what buddies do and what bullies do. Read each statement. If it describes a buddy, circle in the happy face. If it describes a bully, circle in the sad face.

Statement	Buddy 😊	Bully ☹
Great at sharing	😊	☹
Don't like to share	😊	☹
Respectful and kind	😊	☹
Teases and call names	😊	☹
Uses teamwork	😊	☹
Laugh when someone is hurt	😊	☹
Plays with everyone	😊	☹
Pushes, kick and shouts at others	😊	☹
Very helpful and friendly	😊	☹
Work hard at making others look bad	😊	☹

Activity 7
Words to Live By Word Finder Puzzle

Let's see if you can find all the words that are words to live by.
Search for the words listed beside the puzzle, and circle the words you find. Have fun!

```
C O U R A G E O U S F Q A R
P D B E S D B T F T H O P E
K C O S L O V E U R E S O S
I O L P F R I E N D L Y L P
N N D E R T N G X N P R O E
D D B C A R I N G X F E G C
Q A X T L K S G K H U L Y T
G R L I K A B L E A L I I F
H I V L A L M X V P A A A U
T N Z E B R A V E P G B A L
Z G B E L I E V E Y Y L Z R
G V T E A M W O R K A E I N
Y H O N E S T X J O Y F U L
```

~~Honest~~
Courageous
Respect
Kind
Love
Brave
Caring
Helpful
Teamwork
Friendly
Happy
Apology
Bold
Daring
Believe
Hope
Joyful
Fun
Likable
Reliable
Respectful

Activity 8
Being a Good Friend

I can be a
GOOD FRIEND

List the ways in which you can be a good friend, then color in the picture.

Activity 9
Although We Are Different!

No two people are the same but yet there are things that they can enjoy doing together. In this activity, draw and list how you and your friend are different and what you both enjoy doing together.

Me

My Friend

Activity 10
No Bullies Here

Now that you've learnt a lot about Bulling lets recap...

What is a bully?

Identify some bully behaviours:

What can you do to stop bullying?

Write three (3) classroom rules that prevent bullying:

1.
2.
3.

What consequences should be in place for somebody that bullies?

Write a do's and Don'ts list to prevent bullying.

Activity 11
5 Things You Can Do If You're Being Bullied

Here is a list of five things that you can do if you are being bullied. Can you add any of your own ideas to this list?

- Stand up straight and say, "Leave me alone!"
- Hold your hand out and say, "Stop it!"
- Move away to a crowded area.
- Talk to a teacher, parent or friend.
- Stay calm, and talk friendly.

Activity 12
Your Personal Declaration

Now that you've learn about being a bully and being bullied you have the chance to help make the world better. Write down what you can do to help stop Bullying.

Together we CAN stomp out bullying!

Today I am committing to stomping out bullying.

Name: _____

Here's what I will do:

_____
_____
_____
_____
_____
_____

Signed by: _____

Want more great reading?
Check out these books in our series!

Juniper and Rose

"Check out our Dara Publishing Store at
www.darapublishingstore.co
for our children's books, clothing, and much more.."

Strictly Essentials Styles by DARA

  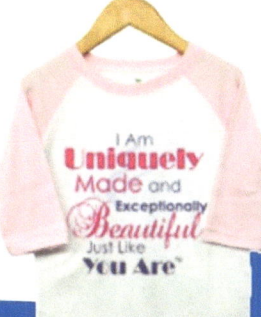 

Visit our website for more: https:www.darapublishing.co/strictly-essentials/

Dara Wisdom and Empowerment Coaching